Does It Look Like Her?

Poems

Melanie Faith

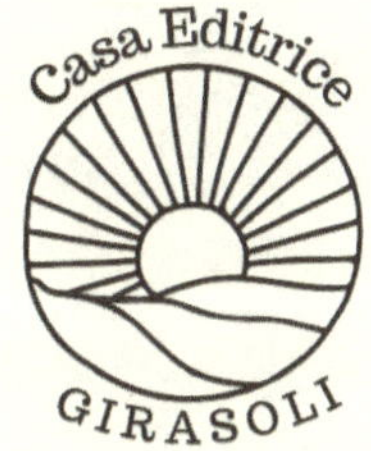

for poets and visual artists

who invest much energy, vision, and care into craft—

create on

Does It Look Like Her?

Published by Casa Editrice Girasoli

ISBN: 978-1-7364077-0-7

First Edition

***

Cover photography by Melanie Faith
Poet's website at: https://www.melaniedfaith.com/

Contents

Part One

Part Two

Part Three

Reader's Guide

Part One

Art Fair

a barebones cabin
last night was sickle moonlight, I took a drive
I'm just trying to make a concert out of it

it's very good you are where you are
today: a canopy with paintings in the sun, open-air
I took home the canvas of the floating arm, palm open

I carried it in both hands like a heavy sack of groceries
I wonder if you'd like me here

Sublet

Somebody else's umbrella. It's upside-
    down. And open. On a hook
    by the door. But so what?

It'll rain again,
    just maybe not today. Maybe
    on the day you forget

to take it with you on errands on foot.
    Pepper pots on the windowsill
    in polka-dot planters, also

a hot water bottle for
    last season's aches and pains.
    The previous tenant's

curtains
    might not be the color or
    the material you like best,

a kind of pink-yellow swim, not
    a pattern you know by name
    or by memory. Before you've left,

you will make your own meaning at last
    with this stuff someone you'll never meet
    has left before you.

Self-Portrait

What do you think of
when you sit there

on the hard chair
with rungs at your back

like iron bars?
You don't think

of anything more
than that you want

that reaction you can't predict,
that little "ah"

of something taken off in the heart motor,
energy in the spine, along fine hairs at the nape,

it's something gold leaf
about you that a mirror won't pick up. If it doesn't

appear,
you can always do over. You do

over and over.
The first attempt is not usually it at all. This doesn't

deter you. This, too, is a part of it, a part of you
that catalysts

that intake of breath,
different than the ordinary pulse. What you are after:

It's the phosphorescence sent swirling
in a firefly jar, that first bright blink—

surprise, lightning.

Birthday 47

"Surprise! Happy birthday, Mommy!"
Sam is a fifty-five pound missile
of happiness bouncing
onto her mattress at 5:12 am. "Look!
You gotta come see. I made you breakfast!" *Uh-oh.*

On Alix's invisible list of what she'd like to do most
for her birthday: sleeping in; painting
in the studio for three, maybe four, unhurried
hours; a leisurely, late dinner at Palmettry's
(there's been no money for luxuries since the split).

"You did?" she blinks bleary, sleepy eyes,
attempts making her voice cheery.

She
fumbles for her glasses in their case, barely gets them on
as Sam yanks her other arm, leading her
into the kitchen nook. She can't help but notice

there is cinnamon sugar trailing from the counter
to the cheap linoleum floor. There's
a splash of milk on the cheap
plastic tablecloth she got for a buck at Goodwill and tried
to pretty up with a vase in the center. It almost worked.

"I made you
sugar toast like Katie showed me how!" Alix's stomach clenches
        at that vile name, at his dad's new flame, but
    she hears herself say brightly, "That's awesome, Sam.

You shouldn't have." The toaster is still plugged in and at least
        he didn't set the kitchen on fire, even if
    the bread bag is gaping open for flies. "It looks delicious.

Here, let me take a bite." Although she has
        zero appetite, she digs in
    as if genuinely hungry. She *mmm*s
            chewing the already stone-cold bread. Sam nods,

            scrutinizes her face as her jaw works the
gritty
        and bitter toast, more cinnamon than sugar. "Yum!"
        Sam's wobbly-toothed grin the best present she gets.

            "This is the absolute greatest
birthday toast I've ever had." And her first.

Ah, hello.

This message is for the inimitable and ultra-memorable Alix [chuckle]. I've been trying to get in touch with you. Meghan had your number—sorry, I know it's been a few months. I'm awful at keeping in touch with people—studio life is just, call me a hermit [chuckle]. Anyway, listen, the painting I made, what, 10 months or so ago after the party?, well, it's been accepted into a juried show, so, yeah, that's great news, right? And I just wanted to invite you to the 7th Street Gallery opening. If you're interested, it's Friday the 12th. I'm sure they'll rustle up some nine-buck chuck and snacks, if that sweetens the deal [chuckle]. Okay, well, give me a buzz back, if you want. My number's 444-212-0—never mind, it'll be on your display from this call. I don't know what I'm thinking today. Long night at the studio, clearly [chuckle]. Okey dokey, hope to see you there, and— [end beep].

In Which Alix Decides Not to Paint a Thing That Weekend

She doesn't
even
know where
she could
start.

"You should
join us.
No experience
necessary."
Meghan (with an h)
encourages. "Digging
in dirt is free
therapy."

So Alix fills
the deadly
quiet every other
weekend
when Sam's with
his dad (and *her)*

at the community
garden. The beets
with their rosy pink-
red bulbs dangling
roots

are her favorites.
They have a tangy
metallic earth scent
like a fresh field
after a rain storm.

When she first
brings a few
home
in her share box,
she makes a
beautiful
borscht
with a swimming
dollop

of sour cream
that Sam won't touch.
He pours, instead, a heaping bowl
of generic fruity rings.

Closing the box after
so they won't go
stale, she shovels
a half-dozen
from her palm
out of habit. Okay,
not bad,
either.

In Which Alix Decides Not to Attend the Opening Night of the 7th Street Show

I'm glad for him, I really am.
It was flattering, sitting for him, but also
a little terrifying.
I want to make my own paintings,
after all. Do I really need to know
how someone else sees me?
Even someone so talented.

I thought about it, asked friends about it,
thought about it again. I should want to
walk in there and stand beside it. I should
want to gauge the reactions of the room,
but I've already been through enough
this year. James' sudden move, the sublet,
starting night classes to finish my degree,
James texting *I'm seeking 50/50 custody.*

What if
this painting doesn't look anything
like me?   Or someone asks me
if I like it and I don't? Or maybe
it's worse if no one
realizes it's me? If it's better or prettier?
Or, worse: What if
        it's a hot mess and looks
like I feel   a lot more than
I'd care to admit? Iffy. I guess what I mean is:

the painting's got a life of its own
now. I've got my own.

In Which Alix Decides, After All, to Attend the 7th Street Art Opening

My breath caught, the room felt stuffy. It was
me, but then again   *not me.*
I didn't know how to feel about that;
I still don't. It's flattering, but then
it doesn't exactly feel personal, so there's *that.*

Nobody standing nearby at the cheese platter,
nobody gathering in clumps
around the gallery, connected the painting to me
in particular; they were all preoccupied
laughing, touching arms, smiling,

walking away.   It was not the first time
since the separation I turned
to share the moment
and found nobody.   At the door, though,
a few minutes later: Meghan,
my in-a-pinch babysitter and true-blue co-
worker, had brought Sam with her.
"Thought you might want a little company,"
Meghan said. Sometimes, after all, things turn out,
I realized, afraid to lean into that moment's grace.

Sam Speaks of *Demeter*, the Famous Portrait of His Mother, Part One

Age 8:
My mommy
is in this picture
in a museum
that this man painted.
It's kind of a big deal.
He's a *real* artist.
Last week, we went
to see it. It was kind of funny
to see Mommy's face
there on the wall. I waved
when we walked in, and
Mommy said, "I'm the real one,
over here," and she made
our special scrunched face,
and we laughed about it.

Part Two

Alix's First Self-Portrait: A Study

i.
Making
her first painting

is the exact feeling
as when Mr. Basker

walked around the
pushed-together tables

to check on everyone's
progress

and when he got to hers
he paused

tilted his head, tilted it back again.
Well. We've got a unit

in ceramics next.
And he'd moved on.

Not the worst thing
that happened

to her in seventh grade
or since.

ii.
She stores it
backwards

in the back
of the hall closet,

behind coats
and a Seagram's box

of records from her
best friend's dad.

She never
gets back to it.

The Sitter

Is it different? Yes,
it's different. When you sit
for a photo, it's lightning.
Quick, quick, quick. They take
shots, capture a slight movement, and then
you just shake it out, follow
the next rapid-fire instruction
as they shuffle through numerous options.

When you are painted or drawn
you must hold, hold, hold the pose.
Your nose itches? You get a pain in your hip
or a charley horse? Too bad. You've committed
to the next fifteen minutes like this,
like a giant game of freeze tag and you
up there on your pedestal
are the only one frozen. Do I think of anything up there? Sure.

Sometimes, it's "Can't they turn up the heat?"
or "No scratching. No scratching. No scratching.
Don't think of that itch at all. Think of meeting Amber for coffee
after. Think of the five o'clock meeting
with my advisor. Think of how nice and steamy that
coffee is gonna be in the thick porcelain cup."

Engines

Her left index finger
pauses above the key

[this is minutes yet
until the siren]

when something
pops into her mind:

Why couldn't
you *do it? You could*

try. She thinks of her
son, across town

in his classroom; she
think of her tween niece

across the country.
She can hear their voices,

Why can't you *paint yourself?*
You always tell us

to go for it
[this is slightly fewer minutes

before the siren, down the
street the fire has already

caught, but she doesn't know it,
doesn't have her windows

open]. She flashes to the yellow
door, to buying the poster board

for the Class 3 presentation
at Harold's Art Supply last month. Well,

she guesses she could. She could maybe go
after after-school pick-up, she could

tell Sam it's for a new project. Low key.
That way if it doesn't work out, she can say—

but Sam already knows. He's a perceptive
kid; he already understands

when things don't work out. She won't have
to explain. She can set it up, out of the way.

She doesn't have an easel,
but she can prop it against the wall—

that'll do and save a few bucks. She's
only experimenting.

It's not a big deal. She feels
a beautiful

whistle that escapes her lips, but
maybe she only thinks it's coming from inside

as the big red engines roar
along the curve

on her borrowed road and she turns to the window
to see the crimson smear of their hurrying below.

Time to run,
time to run.

"It's seriously just a painting,"

says nobody. To be
in a painting is to claim space, is to center
your body power, is to open a body

for any and every meaning it could possibly
hold. Hold on— to be in a painting
is to be superimposed with things you do not say

your body means. People will say it means.
People will not let you
live-and-let-live in your own body.

That you have a body in or outside
a painting means
your body will never stop being beset, overlain

as a see-through transparency sheet on a projector
with unendorsed meaning. Meaning
that travels back to other bodies: the garden, the cave,

the dinosaurs, meaning that blasts forward
into asteroids and stars, into
unconquered planets.

Alix's First Show of Her Own Work at McCann's Gallery

Meghan (with an h)
attends, so does her landlady,
one or two of the mothers
and a granddad from the Wednesday class
and Alphonse from the Art League,
a few people who are friends
of the gallery owner. Hers
doesn't sell. She'd be lying if she said
just being part of the show was
enough.

Then again, a year or two ago
she never would have imagined
she'd make a painting she'd show
in public and making
that one painting had made her want
to never stop making. 47 isn't young,
but it's far from over. Far from

done. She's got a few free hours tomorrow
while Sam's at school and an appointment
with herself. At home,
she's got a blank canvas that won't be blank
for long. She's already got the sketches
in her sketchbook: a side profile of Sam.
She plans to paint his shirt cadmium red
to highlight the glowing life in his face.

Gouache

there's debate
even about
how to say it

there's the GWA-sh camp
and then also
the GOO-ash contingent

that it is malleable
and it is vivid, voltage color
and it is wet

no one contests

It Didn't Quite Take

You think, "Hey,
        if Picasso had his Blue Period
            and his Rose Period
and everybody respects Picasso, then

        why can't I?" Right? Imitation's
    the sincerest form of flattery and all that. So,
I tried with a Purple Period. That got eviscerated.
    Okay, so pink is too close to red, but
        I gave it a go with yellow. Then white.
You know how everybody always crows over

            white space

            white space this
            white space that
            you need more
            white space
            how important
            it is to have. Well,

not in my paintings. What I got out of the whole thing:

just do whatever you need to do. No matter what you do
        somebody's going to call it derivative.

Does It Look Like Her?

Alix's Ex, James:

Look, I try not to say bad things
about the mother of my son.
It's not good for Sam.
But I will say: it's just the kind of
hare-brained thing
Alix would get mixed up in.
Have I seen it? Yes.
After Sam said he and his mom
went to some exhibit, I almost
had to. She certainly didn't run it by me
like the custody moderator said
she's supposed to with these
decisions that affect our son.
Honestly, her shoulders
are all out of proportion
to her head, and the light's
too bright. But I guess
he got one thing exactly right:
this cute little thing she does
sometimes that's half-squint,
half-smirk, makes you want to know
what comes next. That's what got me
back before I knew her.

Sam Speaks of *Demeter*, the Famous Portrait of His Mother, Part Two

Age 20:
When my professor put it
in the presentation for my
Art History class, I slunk down
in my auditorium seat. Contemporary
art, yeah right. That's my *mom*
up there, dude. How'd that make you feel
if it was *your* mom? Weirded out, man.
Weirded out! Don't even
talk about it. Hey,
you going to Stingray's gig on Friday?
Yeah, I'm cutting out early to make
the drive down.

Every poem, every painting

needs a focus
not so much
a theme but
a longing

of the maker
to connect

an idea with
an ideal audience
an idea with
self as audience

Part Three

Does It Look Like Her?

Meghan (with an h):

Oh, I think it definitely
does. Yes. It's just beautiful,
just like my friend!
Eyes, shoulders,
nose, all of her very
flattering, very inviting. Just:
the spiral curls I take
as artistic
license. But it all works;
it gives you her kind,
upbeat personality.

Twelve Years

this is what they call
an overnight success
in the write-up.

When she made her first paintings
her son was in elementary school,
not sophomore year of college.

When she made the first painting
the divorce was a few mere months ago,
now she's been with Alphonse so long

his granddaughter calls her Nonna.
When she first made the painting
she was so unsure—

of herself, of this medium, of creating
anything beyond an investment in Sam.
Now she's sure that her spinach omelet

is her best dish (Sam requests it
when she can get him to come home, that is),
that everything evolves and she'll land on her feet

eventually.
That she's meant to make for others,
that making makes her own life.

Does it Look Like Her?

Sam's Teacher:

Well, not really. Not
that I know her well. She seems
like a very lovely woman, though. Like
the other parents, she volunteers;
she brought in vanilla cupcakes
last month for Sam's special day.
But would I know it was her
in the painting if I *hadn't* already known?
Well, no, sorry. The woman in the painting
seems taller or something. [Whispers:] Maybe
younger? Sorry, I didn't mean
for that to sound mean or whatever.
I'm certainly not an expert on art.

Does It Look Like Her?

7th-Street-Show Attendee:

How do you even
see a figure
through those squiggles? I don't
get it.

. . .
. . .
. . .

Oh. Those are part of her
shoulders? Well,
maybe. If I really
squint
and think about it
that way.

Sam Speaks of *Demeter*, the Famous Portrait of His Mother, Part Three

Age 39:
She looks so young,
so open still. Look
at the searching in her eyes.
The painter got that exactly
right. It would have been
a few months after Dad
left. It must have been hard
for her. We moved into this
duplex that had a sharp curve
in the road right before the turnoff.
There were lots of kids to play
with, and her friend Meghan
lived not too far off—we'd go
to the library a lot, Mom
always had to have her books,
and to the park by the college
sometimes. But overall,
she was never happy there.

Alix Encourages a Discouraged Student Who Stays After Class at the Art League

it's okay
to be tired
of it all and
yet to keep
showing up

in fact, what
they don't
tell you is
we all do,
it's how we get
to a breakthrough

Why You Love Her

Imagine a painting
on a wall above a sofa
where you cannot recall later
if the sofa was gray, bright,
plain or a floral or striped or
if it had any pattern
or pillows. Imagine a figure
so occupying your senses:

a woman, middle-aged, beginning
to soften at the mouth,
her eyelids a little sleepy, her neck
starting to striate with pin-fine lines
you barely notice. Her eyes are alert,
her chin slightly resistant. A woman
prepared.

Reader's Guide

Additional Reading Suggestions:

Books about Painters:

Mary Gabriel's *Ninth Street Women: Lee Krasner, Elaine de Kooning, Grace Hartigan, Joan Mitchell, and Helen Frankenthaler: Five Painters and the Movement That Changed Modern Art*

Roxana Robinson's *Georgia O'Keeffe: A Life*

Books for Writers/Writing:

Natalie Goldberg's *Writing Down the Bones: Freeing the Writer Within*

Anne Lamott's *Bird by Bird: Some Instructions on Writing and Life*

Questions for Discussion, Reflection, or Journaling:

1. Alix is at a fork in the road. Some changes in her life are ones she picked and others aren't. Her only choice is forward. How does she handle this massive amount of change? How have you handled change?

2. Many books about emerging artists have protagonists in their teens or twenties, but Alix is significantly older. What might Alix's life experiences bring to her art? What specific challenges might she face? What does it mean to be a beginner at any age? If you could begin something new to you, what would it be?

3. The bond between Alix and her son is a key relationship in her life that is unwavering. How does Sam's perception of both his mother and the painting change over time? Or does it? What does 39-year-old Sam notice in the painting? Why do you think this is?

4. The painting that the artist makes of Alix is never fully described, save for a few small visual details, allowing readers to imagine their own mind's-eye image of the portrait. Several characters give their opinion of whether or not the painting looks like her or not. What informs each viewer's opinion? What informs your own opinions when considering or judging art? Is the artist's or the viewer's perception most important when viewing art?

5. Alix begins teaching other artists as part of her own artistic process. What did you think about her advice to her discouraged student? What advice would you give to a fellow creator having a hard time? Are teaching and art-making both creative? In what ways?

6. Meghan seems to be a supportive, true friend to Alix. What kind of friend do you think Alix is? What stresses might impact Alix's ability to give back equally to a friend? Who has been a loyal friend to you? Text, call, or email your appreciation for this support.

7. In what ways do artists form communities and share with each other? How important or unimportant is building camaraderie with other artists? How do artists balance alone time to get their work done with time together?

8. What does middle age mean to you? Has your perception of it changed as you've aged or evolved?

9. Who is your favorite character? Which character might be misunderstood?

10. While several serious themes are explored, including ambition later in life, there is also some humor woven into the poems. What did you think about the voice-mail message the artist leaves for Alix in "Ah, hello."? When have you left a bumbling or confused message or said something verbally that you wished you could retract? What part of that experience now strikes you as humorous?

Acknowledgments:

Many thanks to Christine Tierney, Terri McCord, Antonia Albany, Courtney Burger, Laurie Miller, Gina Troisi, Jessie Carty, Angela Mackintosh, Kate Bradley-Ferrall, Ian M. Rogers, Charles A. Swanson, Christin Rice, Marcia Peterson, and Elaina Battista-Parsons who offered encouragement and/or read these poems when they were in-progress. Thanks to Suspended Magazine where my cover photo first appeared and to Jason Anderson at Polgarus Studio for exceptional patience and assistance with my numerous formatting questions, ensuring beautiful and easy-to-read text within my book. Thanks also to the many additional artistic friends and students who asked what I was working on and who offered kind words that also kept me motivated as the poems took on a life of their own and to anyone who offered assistance that I have inadvertently omitted.

For my students, my parents, my sister, brother-in-law, and darling nieces whose support and generosity motivate me in my teaching and art-making.

For my readers and generations of fellow artists finding their way in a society not set up for quiet time and reflection and yet, despite numerous pressures and obstacles, still continuing to grow as creative makers. Shine on!

Author Bio:

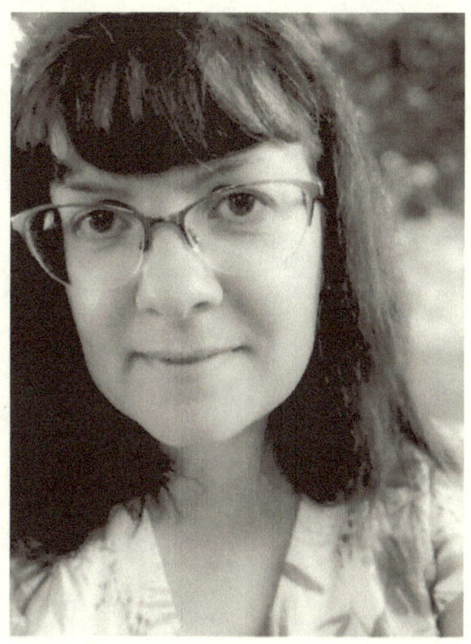

Melanie Faith likes to wear many hats, including as a poet, photographer, prose writer, professor, editor, and tutor. She loves writing about art, the writing process, history, and creativity. She holds an MFA from Queens University of Charlotte. She collects quotes, books, cameras, and twinkly costume-jewelry pins, and she enjoys spending time with fellow writers and her nieces. Learn more about her other books, classes, art, and projects at: https://www.melaniedfaith.com/.

Other Books by This Author:

Nonfiction Craft Books for Writers (all by Vine Leaves Press):

From Promising to Published: A Multi-Genre, Insider's Guide to the Publication Process

Writing It Real: Creating an Online Course for Fun and Profit

Writing It Real: Crafting an Online Course for Fun and Profit

In a Flash!: Writing & Publishing Dynamic Flash Prose

Poetry Power: Writing, Editing, & Publishing Dynamic Poetry

Photography for Writers: A Writer's Companion for Image-Making

Flash writing Series Collection: A Writer's Companion for Flash Fiction, Poetry and Image-Making

Poetry Collections & Fiction (various publishers):

This Passing Fever: 1918 Influenza Poems (FutureCycle Press)

Catching the Send-Off Train (poetry, WordRunner eChapbooks)

https://www.echapbook.com/poems/faith/index.html

Here Humble Admirer (pen named, a Regency novella, Untreed Reads and Uncial Press)

To Waken is to Begin (poetry, Aldrich Press)

About the Publisher:

Casa Editrice Girasoli

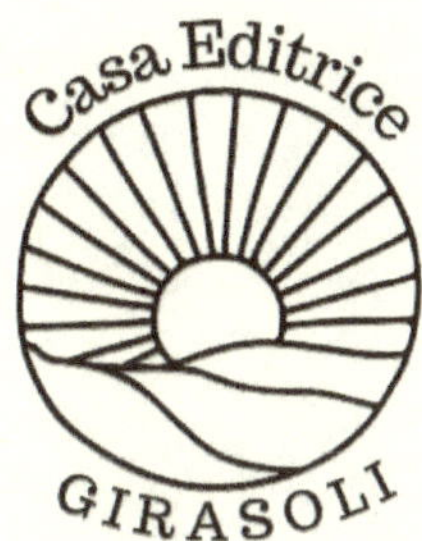

Italian for "Sunflowers Publishing House," the sun-tracking blossom inspires this publisher. As natural heliotropes, sunflowers rise towards the source of sunlight and, late-summer flowers, are often one of the last autumn flowers still growing and standing before first frost. Their petals can range in hues from myriad yellows and oranges to reds, and their size varieties are vast and appear throughout diverse climates worldwide, within at least 80 countries and within all 50 states of the U.S.

While known for their beauty, heartiness, and strength, they are also useful plants. Sunflowers contribute to oil, confections, and various other products, including roasted seeds. They are popular in fields and gardens and often feature in summer and autumnal celebrations and photo shoots.

The ideals of endurance, warmth-seeking and depth, and the natural and imperfect beauty within everyday life underscore the press missions. This is their inaugural project.

www.ingramcontent.com/pod-product-compliance
Lightning Source LLC
LaVergne TN
LVHW050944080826
845145LV00004B/1403

* 9 7 8 1 7 3 6 4 0 7 7 0 7 *